FUN WITH EMBROIDERY

FUN WITH EMBROIDERY

by Jan Beaney

KAYE & WARD · LONDON
in association with Hicks, Smith & Sons
Australia and New Zealand

First published by Nicholas Kaye Ltd under the title
The Young Embroiderer

Copyright © 1966 Nicholas Kaye Ltd

New revised edition published by Kaye & Ward Ltd 1975

Copyright © 1975 Kaye & Ward Ltd

ISBN 0 7182 0093 4

Printed in England by Whitstable Litho,
Straker Bros. Ltd. Whitstable.

Contents

Introduction   7
About Embroidery   8
Your First Thoughts   10
Choosing Threads and Materials   12
Your Equipment   15
Some Useful Stitches   16
Making a Greetings Card   20
How to Begin Designing   21
The Importance of Shapes   22
Choosing your Colour Scheme   25
Appliqué   27
Making an Appliqué Panel   28
Padding   30
Straight Stitches   32
Keeping a Sketchbook   35
Sources of Design – Museums   39
                        The Zoo   40
                        Cut Paper Patterns   43
                        Rubbings   44
                        Textbooks   46
Experimenting with Textures   51
Making a Cushion   53
Stretching and Mounting   54
Embroidcry Yesterday and Today   56
Conclusion   62
Useful Addresses   63
Other Books about Embroidery   63
Acknowledgements   64

By the Watergarden,
Jan Beaney (62 Group),
Applied materials including
cotton, silk, rayon, velvet
and silver tissue. Couching,
straight stitches, french
knots and looped strips of
fabric.

Introduction

This book is about embroidery and how you can learn to be your own designer. If you like a variety of materials, rich colour, texture and pattern, you will find this medium very exciting.

It would be difficult for you to complete an embroidered panel successfully without at first making experiments with shape, colour, texture and stitchery. Therefore, the book is divided into sections, each dealing with an aspect of the subject. You will probably enjoy doing the exercises and if they should be successful in their own right, you could always mount them as cards, calendars or tiny pictures. These colourful decorations, if displayed in your room, could inspire and stimulate you to go on to bigger and better things.

Cut paper patterns.

About Embroidery

Embroidery is a pattern, which can be representative or abstract, carried out on material by means of hand or machined stitchery. Sometimes the basic design is built up by applied materials. The majority of historical embroideries show that the stitch technique used to be of prime importance and in many ways this confined the scope of design. Today embroiderers are going far beyond the old limitations in subjects and materials. As with painting, for some people it is becoming a means of expression.

Embroidery can be used for decorating household articles and dress, or for making pictures, purely as something nice to look at. A scene, an object or part of an object can inspire a design. The main colour, shape or texture of the subject can be over-exaggerated or simplified. As a rule, do not attempt to imitate painting or the precision of a photograph, as the character of the materials and stitchery should show through in a richness of pattern and colour.

It is very thrilling to create your own individual design. Be adventurous and try to make your own pattern without the aid of transfers. Have a look out of the window for ideas. Perhaps a sprig of leaves outlined against the sky, the pattern between the paving stones of your garden path or the centre of an exotic flower could start you off on your very own design.

Sun and Flowers, Jane Taylor (9). Applied fabrics. Stitches include backstitch wheel, straight stitches, couching, knots and buttonhole wheels.

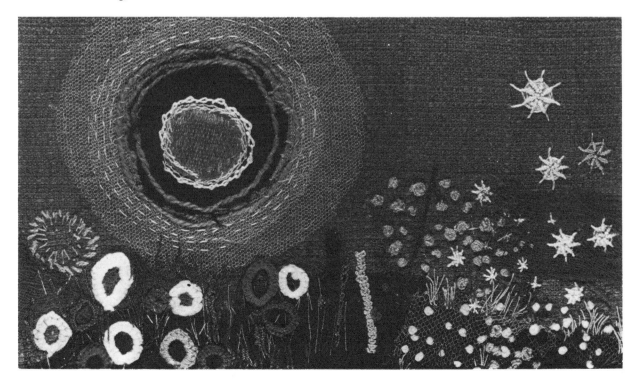

Macivity, Ruth Fox (12).
Storm Clouds, Karen Gogswell (11).

Your First Thoughts

First of all, decide what you want to make. Consider its function, size and shape as this dictates the type of materials, threads and stitches you use.

If the article is to be laundered frequently, as a tray cloth would be, for example, washable fabrics and threads such as cotton or linen are best. If you use a variety of materials there is always the possibility of stretching and shrinking which will cause the embroidery to pucker. When making a cushion, choose a strong, firm material suitable for withstanding wear and tear.

The method of embroidery is also an important factor. An article which is to be constantly handled or washed should have fairly close stitchery. Loose stitches will only catch in the iron or your fingers and would become, in time, mis-shapen.

With purely decorative embroidery such as a picture, there is no need for it to be washed or handled very often. Therefore you can use all sorts of richly coloured and textured materials, threads and stitches. There are no limits, and this style of embroidery is most enjoyable to do.

Detail of whitework skirt border of muslin dress. English 19th Century. Cotton thread, drawn thread work filled in with needlepoint stitches (Victoria and Albert Museum. Crown Copyright).

Batik Landscape, Elaine Evans (15). Batik design enriched with couching and herringbone stitch.

Flowers in a Field, Jean Boyd. Some appliqué. Slubbed knitting yarns, chenille and wools couched. Other stitches include knots, cretan stitch and buttonhole wheels.

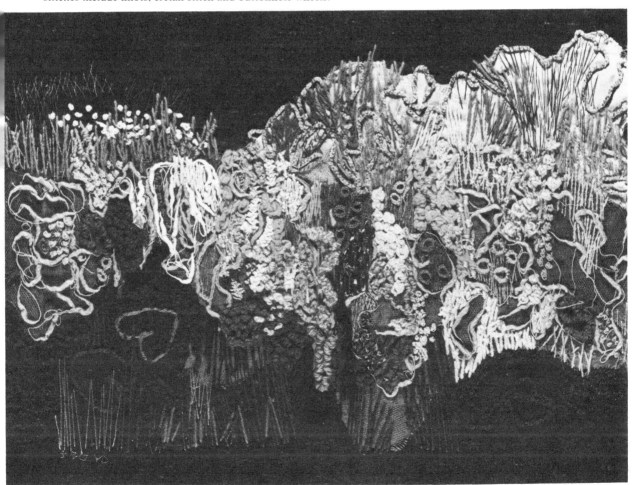

Choosing Threads and Materials

One of the first things you must do is to start your own collection of material and threads. There are a number of interesting matt and shiny threads on the market which vary in thickness. Some are stranded, others are twisted, and they are made in cotton, linen, rayon, silk and wool. Your local shop might only stock one kind of thread so always keep a look out for the embroidery or wool counter of your nearest department store.

There are two important factors to remember. Firstly, choose threads that are in keeping with the material and design. A rug wool would be too heavy for an organdie background and too clumsy for an embroidered device on the pocket of a childs apron. Secondly, do not forget that if your embroidery is decorating an article which is to be washed, choose your threads wisely. Cotton, linen and synthetic threads, and there are quite a number of them to choose from, are a safe choice.

Experiment with a few threads. Select two or three, contrasting thick with thin, smooth with rough, shiny with matt. Do not use them all at once as the effect will be spoilt. Arrange a pattern on the table and when you are pleased with it,

Flowers – glued threads. Helen Green.

Perlita threads and knitting wools glued on to paper to make a motif. Lynne Muir (10).

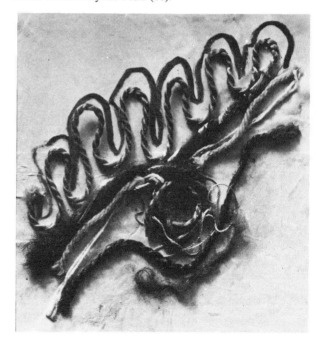

glue the motif on to a piece of material. Sometimes these attractive 'doodles' make very nice cards. If you are doing a free decorative panel, there is no limit to the range of threads you may use. You can collect together all types of knitting wools which may be knobbly or crinkly, or a range of slubbed weaving threads if you are lucky enough to live near a handicraft shop. Other exciting yarns can be metal threads, carpet wools, string, raffia and threads drawn from fabrics such as hessian or tweed.

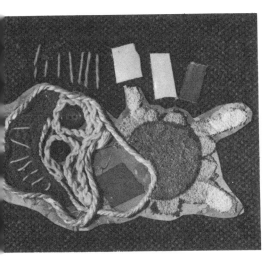

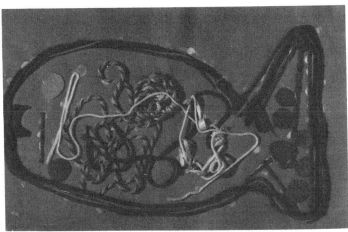

Fish – glued threads, applied felts and wood shavings. Dermot McCaffrey.

Glued motif: fabrics including towelling, paper, string, wool and buttons. Braywood Junior School. (5 and 6).

Glued motif: fabrics including towelling, paper, string, wool and buttons. Braywood Junior School. (5 and 6).

Fish   glued woollen threads. Deborah Coleman.

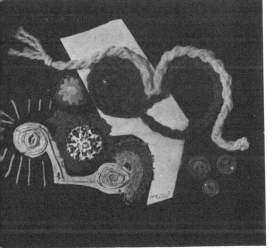

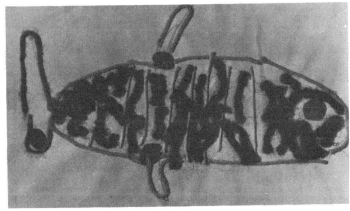

13

You can easily become confused by the vast choice of materials that you can buy these days. Examples are hessian, linen, slubbed rayon, blistered cloque, shot taffeta, rich velvet, lamé nets, and P.V.C. to name only a few.

When you have decided what fabric will be the most suitable for the particular embroidery planned, decide on a colour scheme. If you are doing free embroidery; for example, a picture or a panel, vary the material by choosing rough, medium and smooth textures within your colour plan.

Look out for materials that you can adapt. Some are loosely woven and look very attractive with threads drawn out or pulled into holes to show other material behind.

Train yourself to be observant and to see new materials and their possibilities. Start a rag bag and make your own collection – you will be amazed at how much you will collect from your friends.

Fish – glued and twisted threads, string and wool. Susan Ward (10).

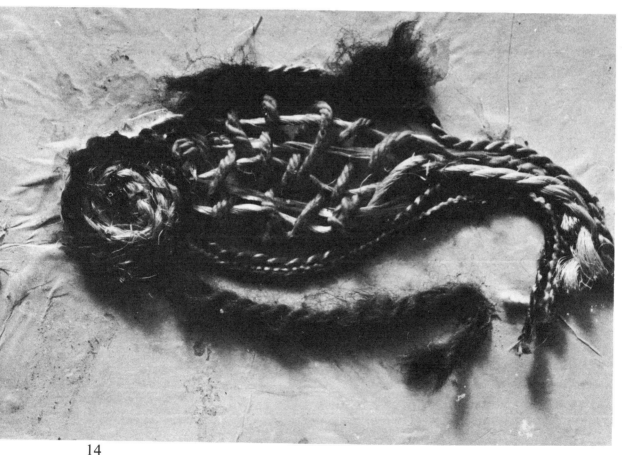

Your Equipment

After you have collected together a variety of materials and threads, you will probably find the following list helpful for the type of embroidery described in this book:

Tape measure

Tacking cotton

Crewel needles in varying sizes, useful for a number of threads:

knitters needles and chenille (larger eye) – for wool on fairly loose weave materials such as hessian.

bead (very fine) – beadwork.

sharps (fine) – tacking; for making up articles.

Thimble

Tailors' chalk or white pencil for marking patterns on material.

Pins.

Scissors

Stiletto – useful for making holes in fabric to ease through thick threads when couching.

Frames – canvas stretcher.

tambour (round). Helpful for when you want to work on material which is taut as in beadwork or straight stitching.

Paints, brushes, pencils and paper for designing.

Tracing paper.

Staple gun.

Drawing pins.

Waves, Diana Harriman (11).

STRAIGHT STITCH This is shown as single spaced stitches worked either in a regular or irregular manner. Sometimes the stitches are of varying size.

COUCHING Lay a thread along line of design and with another thread tie it down at even intervals with a small stitch into the fabric.

CHAIN STITCH Bring thread out at top of line and hold down with left thumb. Insert needle where it last emerged and bring point out a short distance away. Pull thread through keeping working thread under needle point.

DETACHED CHAIN STITCH Work in the same way as chain stitch but fasten each loop at the foot with a small stitch.

SEEDING This simple filling stitch is composed of small straight stitches of equal length placed at random over the surface as shown on the diagram.

16

Some Useful Stitches

Try some simple experiments, just to gain experience and not for any particular purpose. As you can see by looking at the illustrations, you can make quite a good effect with a few simple stitches. Couching is the first line stitch and is useful for laying the foundation of any embroidery.

Select a piece of material, needle and thread and try some of the stitches shown on the next few pages. When you think you have mastered some of them, make up a small motif of lines and simple shapes combining two or three stitches. Remember to fasten on and off securely with a double stitch on the wrong side of your work.

Never make the mistake of thinking you need to use lots of stitches for creating a successful embroidery. A few well-chosen stitches in a variety of threads can make a rich decoration without it being overcrowded.

TWISTED CHAIN STITCH Commence as for chain stitch but instead of inserting needle into the place from which it emerged, insert it close to last loop and take small slanting stitch coming out on line of design. Pull thread through. Work loops close together.

PEKINESE STITCH Work back stitch and interlace with thread.

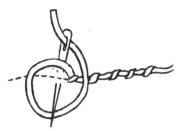

CORAL STITCH Bring thread out at right end of line, lay thread along line of design and hold down with left thumb. Take a small stitch under the line and thread, and pull through bringing needle over lower thread.

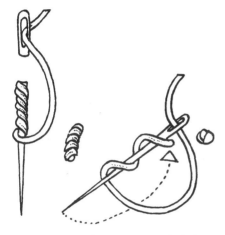

BULLION KNOTS Pick up a back stitch the size of knot required bringing needle point out where it first emerged; do not pull right through fabric. Twist thread round needle point as many times as required to equal space of back stitch. Hold left thumb on coiled thread and pull needle through. Turn needle back and insert again at place where it was first inserted. Pull thread through until knot lies flat.

FRENCH KNOTS Bring thread through. Hold thread down with left thumb and encircle thread twice with needle. Still holding thread, twist needle back to starting point and insert close to where thread first emerged. Pull thread through to back and secure or pass to next knot.

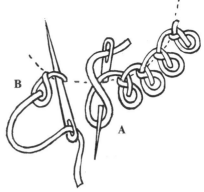

ROSETTE CHAIN STITCH Bring thread through at right end of upper line, pass across to left side and hold down with left thumb. Insert needle into upper line a short distance from where the thread emerged and bring it out just above the lower line, passing thread under needle point (A). Draw needle through and pass under top thread without picking up any fabric (B).

Exercise – first attempt at couching, french knots and buttonhole wheels. Lynda (8).

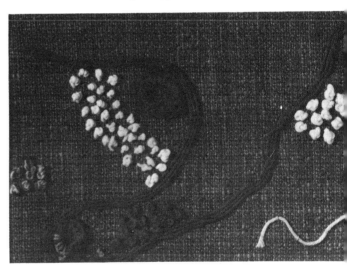

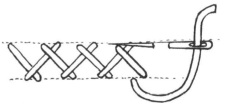

HERRINGBONE STITCH Bring needle out on lower line at left side and insert on upper line a little to the right taking small stitch to left with thread below needle. Next insert needle on lower line a little to the right and take small stitch to the left with thread above needle. Work these two movements alternately.

Detail from *String Ball Doodle*. Prendergast Grammar School. (8-10).

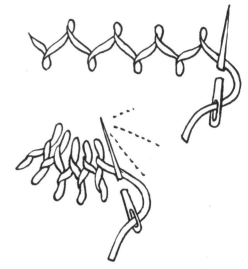

CRETAN STITCH Working from the left bring thread through between upper and lower lines. Insert needle at lower line and make small vertical stitch towards upper line keeping thread to right of needle. Next, insert needle on upper line and make small vertical stitch towards lower line keeping wool to right of needle.

FISHBONE STITCH Bring thread through and make small straight stitch along the centre line of the shape. Bring thread through to right of first stitch. Make a sloping stitch across centre line at base of first stitch. Bring thread through on left side and make a similar sloping stitch to overlap the previous stitch.

SHEAF STITCH Work three straight stitches and hold down with two horizontal stitches.

Some of your more successful stitch 'doodles' will make attractive cards and you could always enrich a motif with a few small beads clustered in the middle or around one of the shapes. Never overdo the beading, and in general select colours that tone in with the main scheme. Contrasting coloured beads and sequins can some-times spoil the look of your work.

For sewing down beads, use a bead needle and a fine but strong thread such as silk. Sequins look at their best if held in place by a small bead, the method being to pass the thread through the material, sequin and bead and back through the sequin and cloth and on to the next one.

18

DOUBLE KNOT STITCH Bring thread through and take small stitch across guide line. Pass needle downwards under surface stitch just made without piercing fabric. With thread under needle pass needle again under first stitch and pull thread through to form a knot. Knots should be spaced evenly and closely to obtain a beading effect.

RAISED CHAIN BAND Work required number of foundation bars which are fairly closely spaced horizontal straight stitches. Bring thread through to the top then pass needle upwards under centre of first bar and to the left. With thread under needle, pass needle downwards to the right and pull up the chain loop thus formed.

FEATHER STITCH Bring needle out at top centre, hold thread down with left thumb, insert needle a little to right on same level and take small stitch down to centre keeping thread under needle point. Insert needle a little to left on same level and take stitch to centre keeping thread under needle point. Work these two movements alternately.

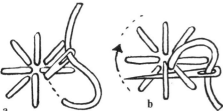

Beside the Lake, Audrey Walker (62 Group). Applied fabrics with some padding. Stitches include french knots and cretan stitch. By courtesy of Kent Education Committee.

BACKSTITCH WHEEL Work eight straight stitches into the centre (a). Bring thread through to the middle and then over and under the stitch behind and on to the next one (b). Repeat until required effect is obtained (c). Fasten off by taking thread over the stitch behind and through to back of material.

19

Greetings card. Upholstery fabric with felt centre. Knots, cretan stitch and straight stitch.

How to make your calendar.

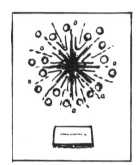

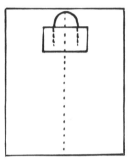

Making a Greetings Card

You will need a piece of card or stiff paper. If you haven't any at home it can be bought from a stationer's shop or an artists' materials suppliers.

Cut it to the size you require and fold carefully in half. Cut out your embroidered motif from the remaining material taking care not to cut too close to the stitches. Trim the ends at the back.

Paste a glue, such as P.V.A. or Copydex, which is suitable for sticking material, evenly over the back. Do not put so much on that it soaks through to the front spoiling the work. Place on the front of the card. The space between the motif and the edge of the card should be very slightly larger at the bottom.

To make a calendar you would need one piece of stiff card, a short length of ribbon and a small calendar. Glue the embroidered motif and calendar carefully in place as described above. Loop the ribbon on the top edge of the card and neatly secure the ends on the wrong side with a small piece of gummed paper – see picture above.

How to Begin Designing

Having determined the method and material of your embroidery, the design is the next stage.

If you keep a sketchbook and a collection of magazine and newspaper cuttings and photographs for reference you will probably have lots of ideas.

There are three main points to remember. Choose a subject or pattern that will be fitting for the purpose of the embroidery. For example, a picture designed for a nursery would not always be suitable for a dining-room.

The second point is, make the design fit the shape of the article to be embroidered.

Thirdly, consider whether the colour scheme is suitable for the particular function of the article.

Detail from wall hanging. Tapestry with stitches overlaid (Humble Oil Refinery, Texas).

Detail from cushion. English late 16th Century. Silver – gilt and silver threads, metal strip and silk in straight stitch and couching (Victoria and Albert Museum. Crown Copyright).

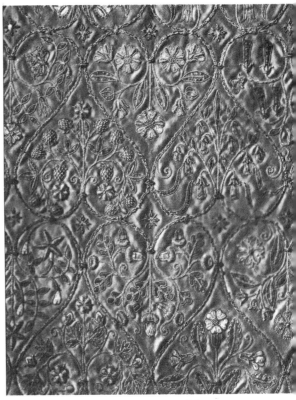

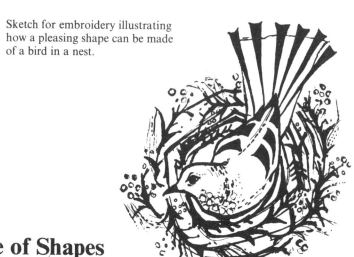

Sketch for embroidery illustrating
how a pleasing shape can be made
of a bird in a nest.

The Importance of Shapes

Allow the design room to expand as the idea develops. Remember to keep the interest in the picture: have a focal point. Everything else in the design should help to emphasize this point, and planning the background spaces is essential. Take care not to have part of a subject such as a figure, a tree or a very light, dark, or vividly coloured shape awkwardly placed on the side of the panel, as the use of this can take your eye away from the focal point.

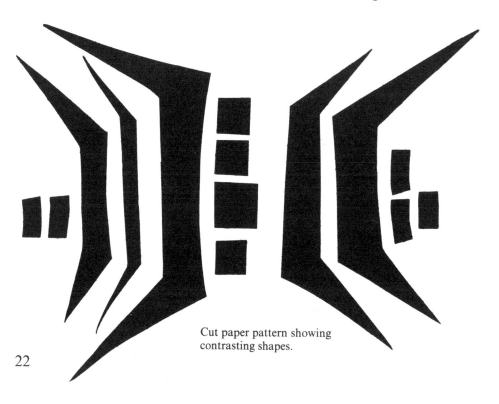

Cut paper pattern showing
contrasting shapes.

Dew pond, Kent, Heather Padfield
(62 Group)

Detail. Skirt border. Crete 1733.
Notice how the repeating patterns
vary in size and shape (Victoria
and Albert Museum. Crown
Copyright).

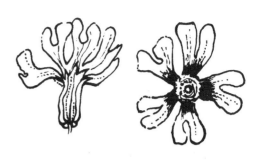

Sketch for embroidery – pink campion. The petal shapes can be interpreted in various ways.

Have big shapes and helping shapes if the motif is to be repeated. Forms of the same size can be boring. Contrasting lines with solid shapes can also help make a pleasing pattern. Make a drawing of a flower and notice the intricate patterns and markings. Simplify these points into a design. Observe how the flower designs illustrated in this book are contrived into certain shapes and how charming they are. The Elizabethans were especially fond of floral devices and embroidered them on many things.

Gloves; English 17th Century. Silk embroidery with couching in metal threads (Victoria and Albert Museum. Crown Copyright).

Woman's tunic; English late 16th Century. Some couched work (Victoria and Albert Museum. Crown Copyright).

Choosing Your Colour Scheme

Always keep a look out for ideas for colour schemes. There are many beautiful colour plans all round you in everyday life. If you look at a vast scene you will be overwhelmed by so many colours that you will not know where to start. Take a close, long look at a detail of that scene. You can collect a lifetime of schemes by training yourself to observe such things as speckling on the back of a toadstool, rain-sodden tree trunks, fading leaves in autumn, subtle-coloured fish scales, wet paving stones or slate tiles, pebbles on a beach, the inside of an oyster shell, oil in a puddle; the list is endless.

However, there are a few safe rules to remember. Never use every colour you can think of in one design. The colour should suit the function of the embroidery. Choose a main colour and then add smaller amounts of helping or complimentary colours in light and dark shades. Embroideries that are carried out in one colour but in varying tones, are often the most successful.

Pink Shell, Susannah Kenton-Smith (11). Applied fabrics, couching in a variety of threads.

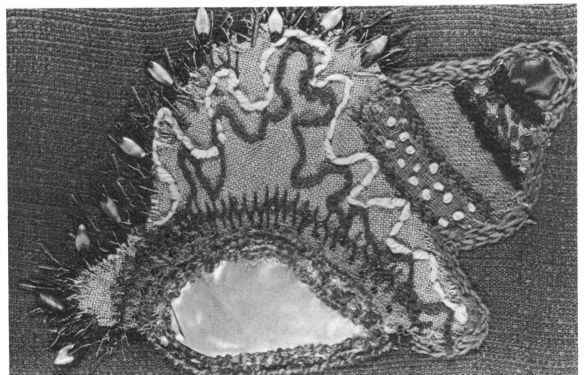

Noah's Ark. Paul Buckley (9).

Dragon, Fiona Spicer (10). Appliqué, couching, knots and running stitches.

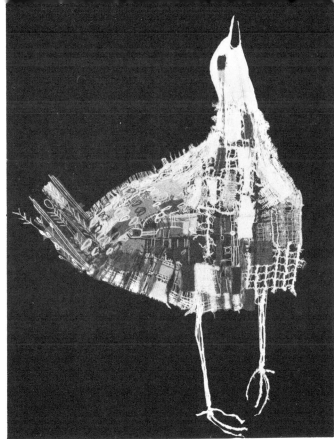

Bird by Pat Ross. The rule of matching warp and weft has been broken here to obtain the feathery back and tail of the seagull.

How to match warp and weft.

Appliqué

Appliqué is the term used for the technique of applying one material on to a background fabric and enriching with stitchery.

If you are making a decorative picture or a motif for a cushion cover using applied pieces of fabric, work out carefully where they are to be placed before sewing down. You can either transfer the design from paper to fabric as described on page 44 or you can draw freely on the material with a white pencil or tailors' chalk if you feel confident enough.

Always remember when applying material to match the way the threads run (the warp and weft as it is called) of both the material to be applied and the background to prevent puckering (see illustration, above left). This rule can be broken if you want a special effect which can only be gained by not matching them. For example, loosely woven material deliberately frayed could be applied in many directions to obtain a feathery appearance. Very rich, yet subtle colour changes can be obtained by applying shot fabrics in varying ways.

Most fabrics should be herringbone stitched or machined to the ground material to prevent the edges fraying. Materials that have been backed with iron-on vilene rarely fray and as with net, leather and felt these can be stitched around the edge with small catch stitches. All stitching should be done with fine thread in a colour to match the material, so that it does not compete with any surface stitching that may follow.

27

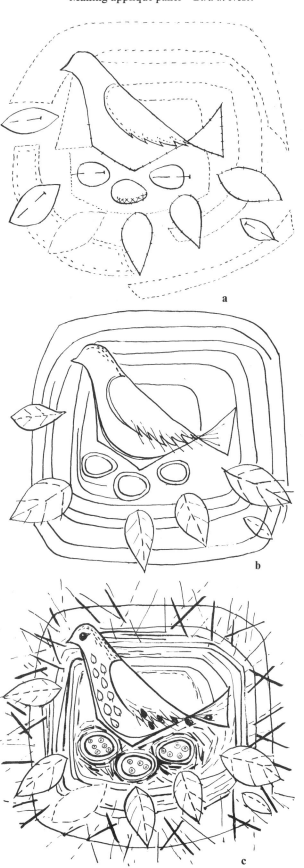

a

b

c

Making an Appliqué Panel

Cut out, in paper, a simple shape, perhaps a bird or flower. The design you have cut out can be used as a pattern for the material you wish to apply. Remember to match the grain of the fabric.

Choose interesting fabrics such as a smooth material to be applied to a textured one. Keep to a simple colour scheme.

Pin the pieces on to a background material, tack and sew down as described (Fig. a).

Develop the main design with line stitches. Sometimes follow the edges of the applied pieces and other times break into the background spaces (Fig. b).

Enrich some areas with textured stitchery (Fig. c).

Emphasize the focal point by using a certain stitch, a spot of intense colour or a change in tone or texture. The motif shown on these pages is worked in wool and cotton but the focal point is made important by the use of a shiny thread, slightly lighter in tone and speckled with tiny beads.

Appliqué panel complete.

Detail from an embroidered picture: *David and Bathsheba*, showing how padding was used in the 17th Century when it was called 'stumpwork'. English 1656 (Victoria and Albert Museum. Crown Copyright).

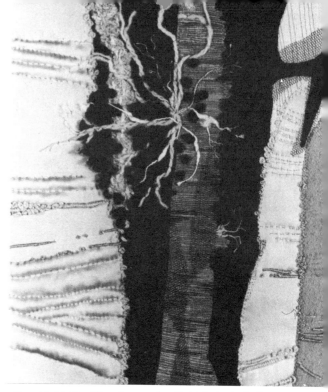

Spanish Fields, Olive James. Applied fabrics include satin, slubbed silk and wool.

Padding

Padding is fun to do and can enrich some designs for free embroidery.

The historical example illustrated was one in the 17th century when the padding often consisted of small blocks of wood covered with white satin. The first method explained here is quite simple and the pad is made of felt.

When you have decided on the size and shape of the intended raised part, cut a piece of felt exactly to the size. Follow with two or three other pieces each the same shape but slightly smaller than the one before (Fig. a). The more layers of felt you use, the more raised the padding will be (Fig. b). Tack the pieces together. Cut out the covering material, the same shape but about $\frac{1}{4}''$ larger all round. Work a small running stitch around the edge (Fig. c). Place the felt filling in the centre of the material and pull the thread tightly so that the material curls itself round the felt. Secure the thread (Fig. d). Apply the pad to the background material by small hem stitches, taking care to tuck in any surplus material as you go (Fig. e).

Method of padding.

a

b

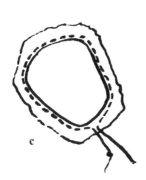

c

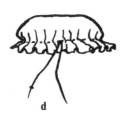

d

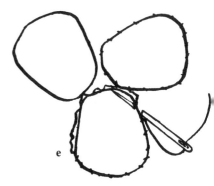

e

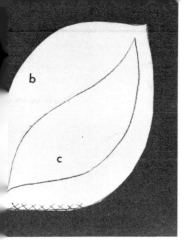 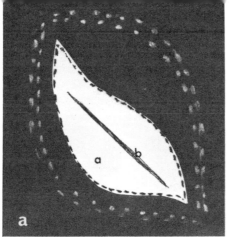 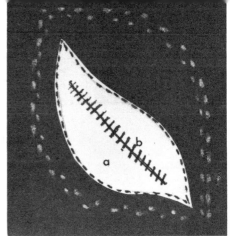

Front:
(a) Background fabric.
(b) Applied fabric.
(c) Shape to be padded
  marked out.

Back view:
(a) Shape backstitched.
(b) Cut is made taking care
  not to cut backstitches or
  front layer of fabric.

Back view:
(a) The padded shape.
(b) The slit is sewn up after
  inserting the cotton wool.

Another way of padding is by inserting the stuffing from the back of the work. First you need to apply a layer of material to the background fabric. After deciding the shape of the area to be padded, mark with a white pencil or tailors' chalk. Work a backstitch around the shape taking care to stitch through both fabrics (Above, left). On completion turn to the wrong side of the stitched shape and carefully cut an opening into the background fabric (Above, centre). Do not cut too near the backstitch or the front layer of material. Shred cotton wool into tiny pieces to avoid lumping and insert into the opening until it looks as raised as you want upon viewing from the front of the embroidery. To finish, oversew the slit (Above, right).

Detail of panel 'Minerva', Jean Baker. Showing examples of padding.

Detail, Anne Vaughan (62 Group). Contrasting shiny and matt surfaces. (Winter Series – Snowed up).

Straight Stitches

Straight stitches can be arranged in many ways giving a wide range of effects. They can be the basis of other rich textural stitchery such as darning, some macramé knotting, buttonhole stitch and areas of raised chain band stitch. Needleweaving can also be worked over straight stitches, perhaps using fine shiny threads over matt ones, giving interesting results. (See page 55).

Straight stitches worked in groups or singly can help to give the impression of movement in a design. They can be placed to accentuate the applied shapes or existing stitchery and can often soften the hard edges of the design without intruding upon it.

If straight stitches are worked in a variety of directions in the same colour in a fine shiny thread, such as silk or machine thread, differing light effects will change the colours and tones very slightly giving a richer surface without it being too obvious.

Detail from panel *By the Watergarden*, Jan Beaney (62 Group), showing straight stitches and couched wools and cords.

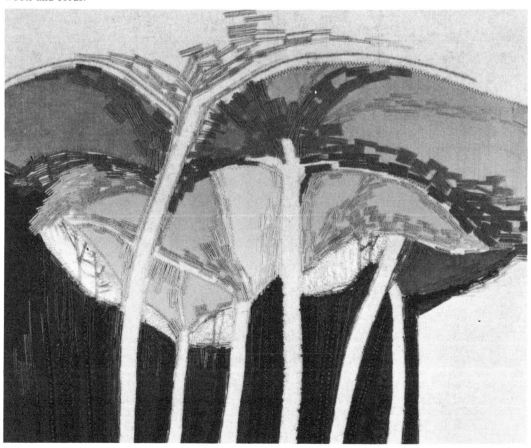

Stephenson's Rocket, Mark Lister (11).

Birds and Beasts, Margaret Eaton (11).

Winter Cottage, Anne Vaughan (62 Group).

Stone, Beryl Tilley. Applied fabrics including nets, couching and knots.

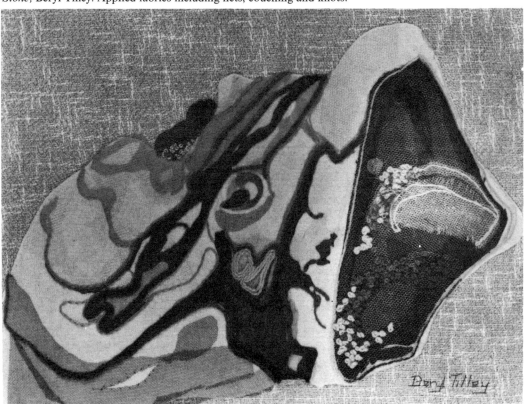

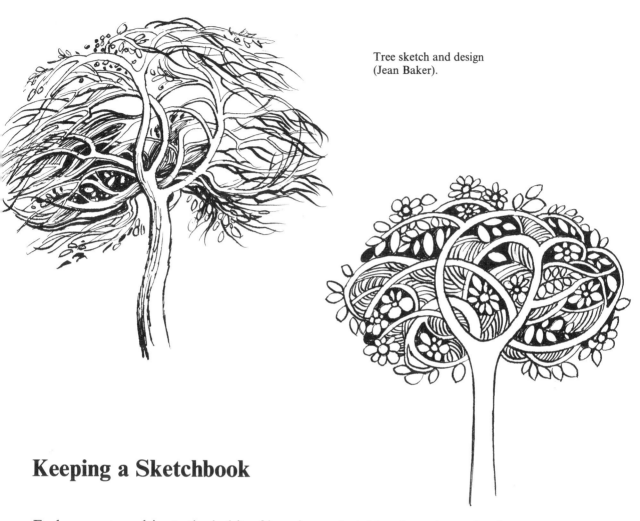

Tree sketch and design
(Jean Baker).

Keeping a Sketchbook

Endeavour to cultivate the habit of keeping a sketchbook, as it can be the source of many pleasing designs. Take notice of anything that catches your eye whether it is a scene, a peculiar shape of tree, a group of pebbles on a beach or the pattern of sweets in a jar. Do not become too disheartened if your sketches are not easily recognisable at first. You will improve with regular practice. When beginning a sketch, always take note of the proportions of one thing to another and the shape and size of the spaces between the objects. First draw a rough sketch remembering these points and then add details and an indication of textures. (See book list).

When you have collected some examples look carefully at your subjects. Pick out one you like and consider it in terms of pattern, material and stitches as described on pages 10 and 12.

Simplify or emphasize any parts you wish.

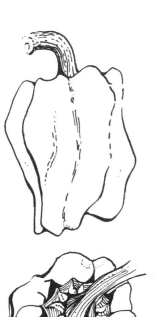

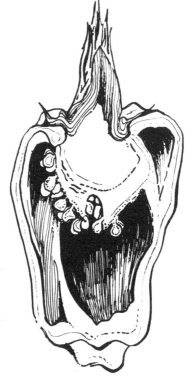

Sketches. *Green Peppers.*

Group of Trees, Kent. Heather Padfield (62 Group).

36

(a) Sketch of Honeysuckle. *(b)* Motif from shapes between flowers.

The design on this page has been made from the sketch of a plant. The spaces between the stems and flowers make the pattern, not the flower itself.

Sydney Opera House, Vivien Horler (15). Couching and filling. Stitches in wool and metalised threads. Padded patches.

Sketch of a pendant.

Design – adapted from eagle taken from Egyptian panel.

Detail from panel *Minerva*, Jean Baker.

Bird – detail from border. Chinese (Embroiderers Guild Collection).

38

Sea urchin design;
West Indies.

Sources of Design: Museums

You can gather together many exciting designs by visiting and sketching in a museum.

When looking at natural forms or patterns from the work of craftsmen of the past you will find a wealth of ideas.

Having discovered something you like, perhaps from a finely modelled ship, a marine creature or a pendant, copy the basic character of the pattern. When using the motif in an embroidery you can make colour and texture variations or emphasize one part more than another.

Your ideas might develop into a repeat pattern for bead embroidery, a decorative hanging or a design for a cushion. The possibilities are endless.

Detail of skirt border. Crete 18th Century. Linen embroidery with silk in cretan, feather and herringbone stitches (Victoria and Albert Museum. Crown Copyright).

The Zoo

Detail from panel *Old Woman and Bird*. Hand and machine embroidery. Audrey Tucker (62 Group).

Elephant – detail from border. Chinese (Embroiderers Guild Collection).

There are many exciting subjects to be seen at the zoo – lions and tigers, owls and flamingos, angel fish and turtles and so many other creatures.

If you take photographs or make drawings of any of them, look and see if they are marked in such a way that you can make the pattern much bolder when turning the subject into an embroidery design. If you look at the photographs in this section you will see how other people have interpreted this. The rough patchy skin of a rhinoceros is shown by applying buttons, beads and pieces of wood. The owl's feathery breast is exaggerated by looping stitches in a variety of threads and the lion's mane is represented by loosely hanging threads. You can still identify these creatures but they have been made to look more decorative.

Why not choose an animal or bird that you like and use it as the basis for an appliqué picture for your room?

Rhinoceros, Betty Fraser.

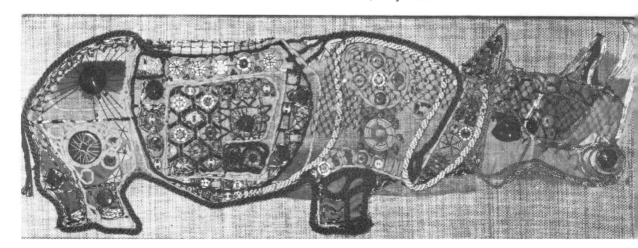

Marmaduke swims the Channel, Dawn Self, Gloria Kendall (14).

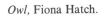*Owl*, Fiona Hatch.   *Lion*, Diane Wade (11).

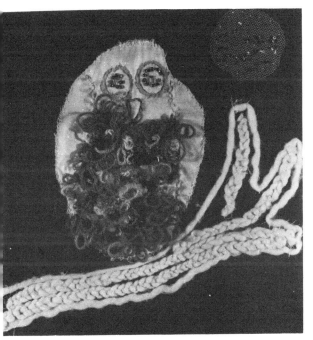

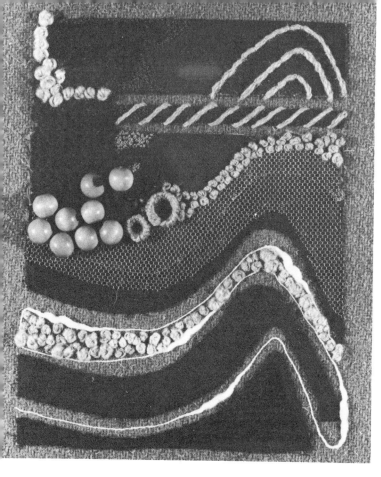

Cut paper pattern.

Panel by Hilary Conboy. Applied fabrics, shisha glass, knots and areas of raised chain band stitch.

Panel by Bridget Gray. Based on cut paper design.

Cut paper pattern.

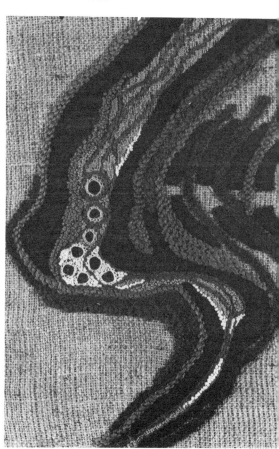

Paper pattern cut out in separate pieces.

Cut Paper Patterns

Cut paper patterns are original and are great fun to do. Find some scrap paper and a pair of paper-cutting scissors and start by cutting out different shapes.

You can fold the paper several times, cut out some shapes and when you open the paper you will find some sort of pattern. If you are not pleased with it, fold it again and cut out some more pieces. Always remember to cut out big pieces and little pieces, as one contrasts with the other.

Another method is to cut out separate pieces and to place one next to the other with small spaces between as shown on this page. Keep to simple shapes and make the background spaces as interesting as the actual paper pieces.

Once the desired pattern is obtained, it is then cut out again in cloth and applied to the background material. Remember to match the warp and weft of both fabrics. You can also pin the paper patterns to the ground material and chalk or tack round the shapes. Having tacked the outline of the design, you can embroider in and around the motif. The design on the opposite page originated from a cut paper pattern.

43

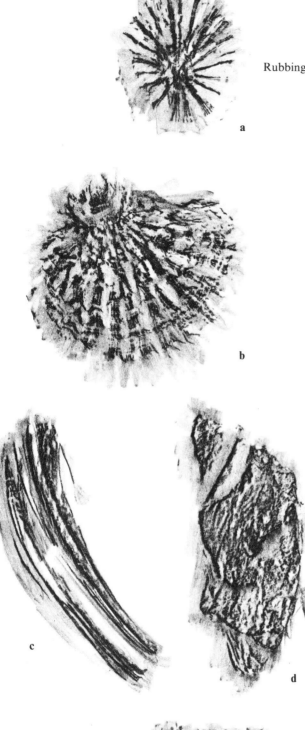

Rubbings: a, shell; b, shell; c, stone; d, slate; e, base of wicker basket

Rubbings

Some people find it very difficult to make abstract designs which are interesting in shape and texture. By taking rubbings from different surfaces, you will collect a wide selection of patterns to choose from. Of course you have to pick out the most interesting part and decide whether it will suit the particular shape of the article to be embroidered. Usually the rubbings vary in tone so you can pick your threads accordingly. The thickness of line can be interpreted by line stitches in a variety of threads.

For making a rubbing you need some thin paper and a black greasy crayon (heelball) or 4B pencil. Place the paper over a surface, perhaps a rough bark of a tree, holding firmly in place, and shade across in one direction. Do not press too hard as the pencil will pierce the paper, nor too lightly as little or no impression will be made.

On collecting some patterns, look carefully at all the shapes and select a part you like. Always look for a main shape or focal point and helping shapes. If the pattern is too small for what you want, copy the design in a larger scale on to another sheet of paper.

When you find you have a particularly pleasing design, copy the main features of it on to your material with a white pencil or tailors' chalk and embroider.

44

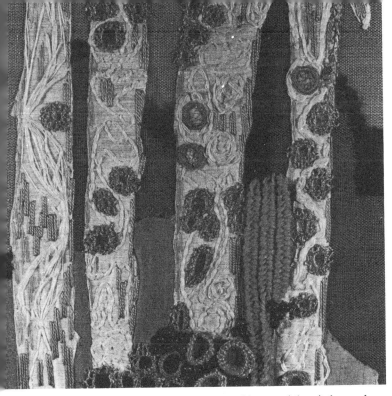

Detail, *Silver Birches* by Joyce Kohn couching, straight stitches and buttonhole rings.

Design showing a variety of strings couched – Gillian Stables (16).

Experimenting with textures. Shapes pulled in loosely woven fabric, knotted cable chain, raised chain band and looping stitches. Olive James.

Bark.

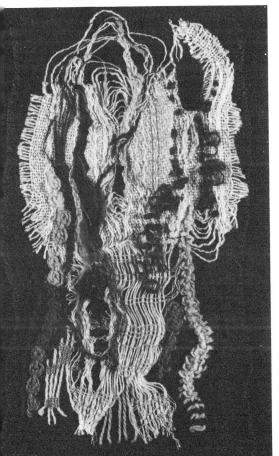

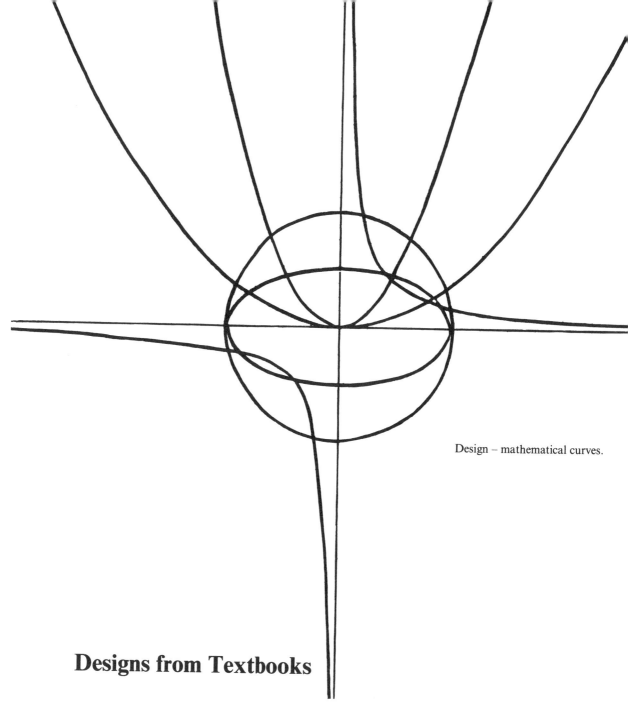

Design – mathematical curves.

Designs from Textbooks

Some exciting designs can be taken from textbooks, especially ones on biology or nature study. If you go to your nearest library and look through one of these books, you will probably find diagrams and photographs of magnified cross sections of leaves and stems and so on. Some of the patterns are very exciting and if used as embroidery designs, in good colour and with a variety of interesting threads, they can be fun to do.

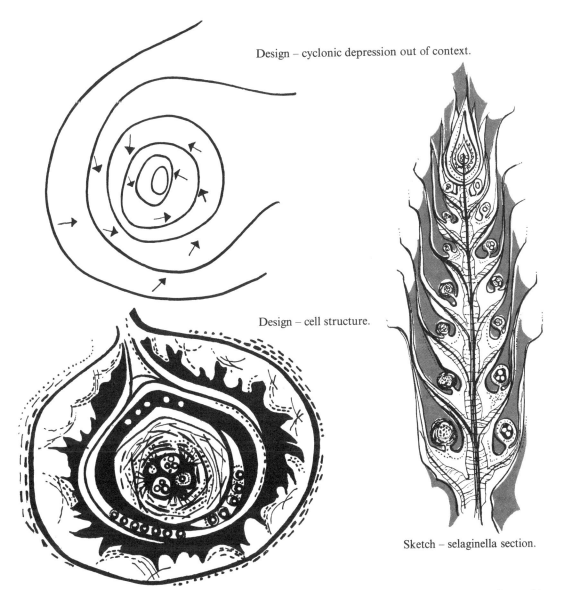

Design – cyclonic depression out of context.

Design – cell structure.

Sketch – selaginella section.

Once you have found a pattern that you like, you need only take a section of it (the part that has the nicest shapes in your opinion) and draw it much larger on to a piece of thin paper – taking care to show the main character of the shapes and the spaces between the shapes. These are very important.

Choose an interesting piece of material for the background and tack your piece of paper firmly onto it tacking also around the main lines of your design. Make sure that you fasten on and off securely.

When this is completed, very gently tear away the piece of paper and the tacking stitches in the drawn design will be left on your material. Having already selected a colour scheme, you can then apply pieces of material in certain parts and contrast with line and filling stitches in varying types of thread in some of the remaining shapes. Never overcrowd the design with too much material or too many stitches. Leave some empty spaces to contrast with others.

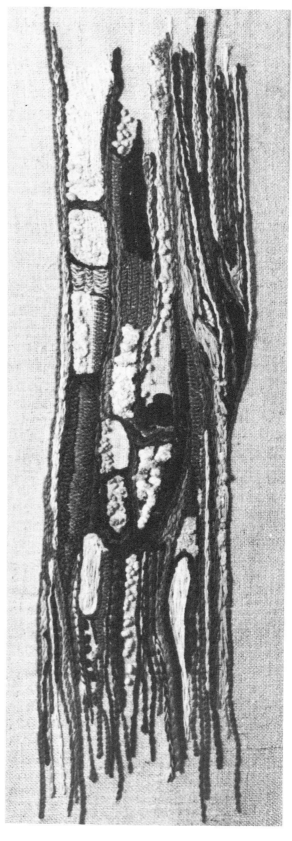

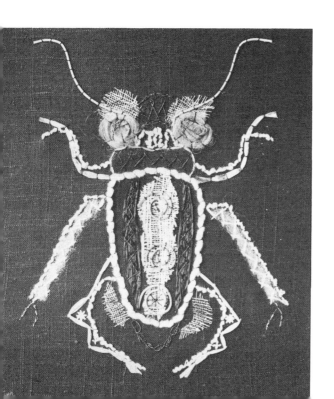

Buttercup Field, Deborah Udall (11).

Far left, top: *Cell Structure*. Stitchery on hessian. Barbara Priest.

Far left, bottom: *Beetle*. Wool, string, thin cane and raffia on linen. Maureen Southey.

Left: *Tree cell one,* Jackie Garner (15).

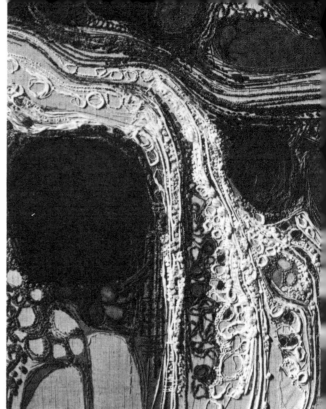

Which way through the magic wood by pupils of Hill Top Middle & Infant School (10).

Waterfall, Audrey Walker (62 Group).
(Victoria and Albert Museum. Crown Copyright).

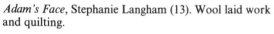

Adam's Face, Stephanie Langham (13). Wool laid work and quilting.

Panel *Golden Fleece*, Julia Caprara (62 Group).

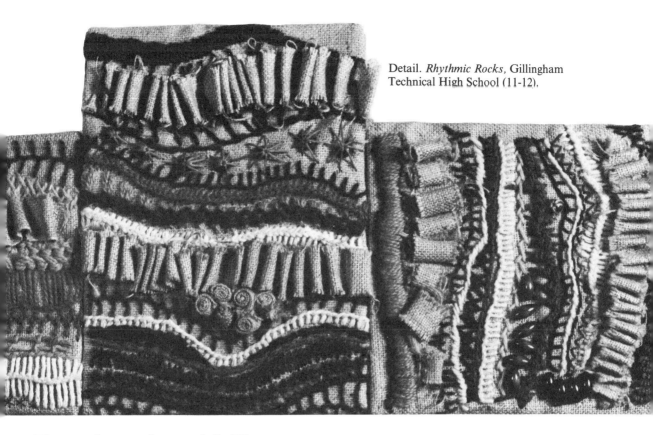

Detail. *Rhythmic Rocks*, Gillingham Technical High School (11-12).

Experimenting with Textures

Try experimenting with materials and threads to achieve interesting textural effects. Contrast the materials you apply. They could be smooth, silky, blistered or rough and loosely woven. Areas of the applied fabric could be cut away to expose the ground material. Nets could be layered, cut away, overlapped both on the applied and ground fabrics to achieve very rich results.

Padded surfaces, especially if the material is of silky texture, can contrast beautifully with a matt or textured background.

Try pleating, rolling, gathering and deliberately puckering the fabric. Some of the indented areas could be encrusted with knotting stitches or clusters of beads. Long strips of fabric or leather can be looped, rolled, frayed or used for forming long stitches. Experimenting with threads and stitchery can also be exciting. Attempt one stitch in a wide variety of threads. For example, contrast couching in: a fancy textured weaving yarn, a slubbed knitting wool and a silky cord. Try french knots, raised chainband and knotted cable chain stitches in a fine perle thread and a very thick rug wool. Interesting results can be obtained by looping threads and leaving loose ends which can also be frayed, plaited or gathered into groups.

51

Panel by Jean Williams showing shiny cords couched and with bullion, french knots and raised chain band stitch.

Panel by Jean Boyd showing appliqué, padding, couching and needleweaving.

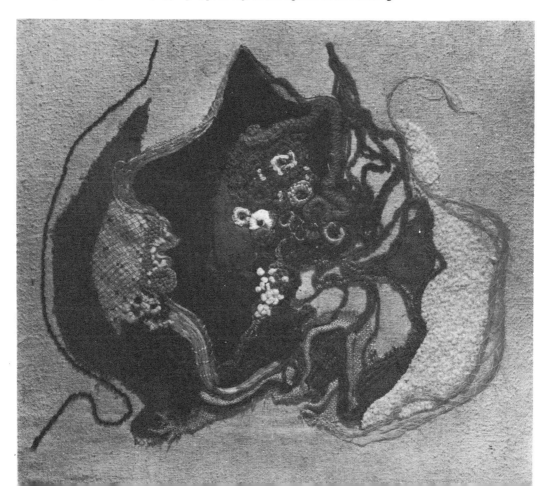

Making a Cushion

When designing for a cushion it is advisable to make the pattern attractive from all angles. Remember to use suitable fabrics and stitchery.

Having decided on the size of the cushion, carefully cut out the matching sides allowing for one inch turnings.

Transfer the design and carry out the embroidery.

Place the right sides of the cushion cover together, tack and machine or back-stitch three sides (Fig. a).

Turn the cover right side out and press.

Cut out a lining case about a $\frac{1}{2}$ inch smaller all round than your cushion cover. Sew together on three sides. Turn inside out and stuff with a suitable filling such as foam rubber or kapok. Sew along the top so that the filling is entirely enclosed. Insert into the cover and slip stitch neatly along the remaining side (Fig. b).

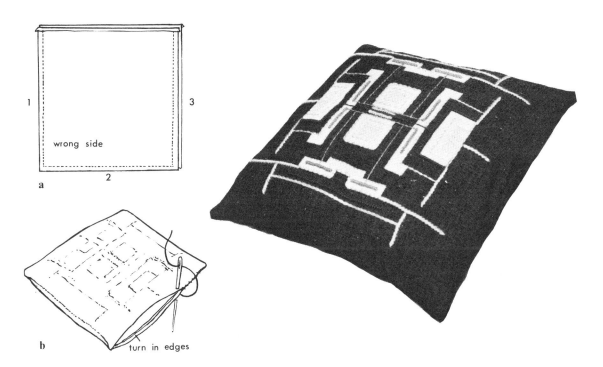

(a) and *(b)* Making a cushion.

Cushion. Christine Nuth. Design from a cut paper pattern.

Stretching and Mounting

Most embroideries, especially panels worked freely in the hand, need to be stretched on completion. All the creases will be removed without the stitchery being flattened as it would be if it was ironed.

You will need a drawing board, drawing pins and two or three layers of blotting paper. Wet the blotting paper and stretch it flat on the board. Place the embroidery wrong side downwards and pin along one side. Repeat the process on the remaining sides pulling the material quite tautly. Make sure that the weave is kept straight in both directions (see above right).

Having stretched your work you will need to mount it if it is going to be a picture.

The materials needed are strawboard or card, a needle and some nylon knitting yarn. Use the firmer strawboard or hardboard if your panel is quite large. Thinner card will do for smaller pieces.

Cut the board to the correct size. Place the embroidery right side downwards on a table and the board on top in the right position. Fold the edges over and pin temporarily in place.

Fasten the thread securely in the centre of one side and then commence lacing from side to side pulling the thread tightly and working from middle to outer edge of each side. Remember to fasten on and off securely each time you need to renew the thread (see right). The panel can now be easily framed.

If the embroidery has been stretched in a

54

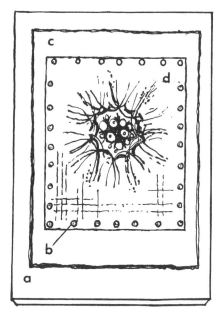

Method of stretching, *(a)* drawing board; *(b)* and *(c)* blotting paper; *(d)* embroidery. Pin round, keeping warp and weft straight.

Method of mounting. *(a)* lace from side to side, middle to outer edge; *(b)* lace from top to bottom, middle to outer edge.

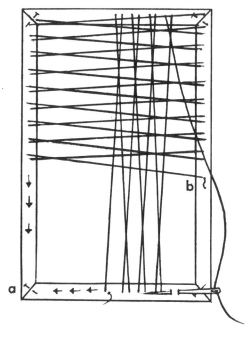

Distant Trees, Jan Beaney (62 Group). Straight stitches, needleweaving, darning and buttonhole stitch.

The Indian, Yuta Marie Macholl.

frame from the beginning of the work, this can be laced over board as described without stretching it on damp paper. Alternatively, the material can be stapled more securely over the existing frame and this then inserted into the picture frame itself.

These days it is not necessary to glaze your work. A fine spray of a fabric protector such as Scotchguard will not alter the appearance of fabrics or threads.

Embroidery Yesterday and Today

It is always interesting to see examples of historical and present day embroidery in the various areas of the medium. You will probably like, and be encouraged by, some aspect of both. Perhaps you can work out from where the embroiderers evolved their ideas. Notice the type of threads, stitches and materials used to give certain effects.

Man's jacket. Hungarian 19th Century. Sheepskin with applied ornaments in coloured leather (Victoria and Albert Museum. Crown Copyright).

Marc Bolan, Lindsay Palmer (16). Stitches include knots and backstitch wheels.

House at Palmela, Audrey Walker (62 Group). Stitches
include seeding, straight stitches, cretan stitch and knots.

Allotment 1, Heather Clarke (62 Group). Hand and machine embroidery and padding.

Metamorphosis, Herta Puls (62 Group). Stretch fabrics and leathers over chipboard plaster and foam.

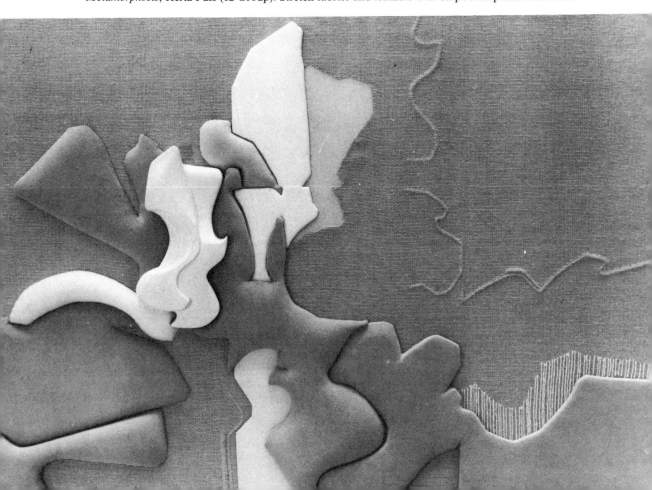

Within the tight limitation of church embroidery, some very stimulating work is being done with rich and unusual materials: the designs seem less stiff and formal. Embroidery on dress is becoming very exciting. Machine embroidery is increasingly popular on undergarments, childrens' clothes, evening wear and creative embroidery. There is a high degree of skill needed for machine embroidery to be wholly successful. However, once mastered, it is a fairly quick method of working and it suits the pace of living today. You will probably find it great fun to do if you ever have the chance to use the right sort of machine. There are a few books listed on pages 63 and 64 which will help you to make a start in this method of embroidery.

Free embroidery today is being accepted much more as an art form. Educational authorities and private collectors are including embroidered panels in their collections. Professional artists have the chance to exhibit their work and are commissioned to work panels and hangings for decorating private apartments and public buildings. Children, teachers and the general public are now showing great interest in this exciting medium.

Detail. Bedspread. Cheryl Welsh (62 Group). Machine embroidery.

Detail of *Syon Cope*. English
late 13th Century. Silver and
silver gilt threads. (Victoria and
Albert Museum. Crown
Copyright).

Dark Centre, Beryl
Chapman (62 Group).

Hand embroidered panel by Audrey Walker (62 Group).
Commissioned by the City of Bath in 1973 to
commemorate 1,000 years of English monarchy
973 – 1973. Pump Room, Bath.

61

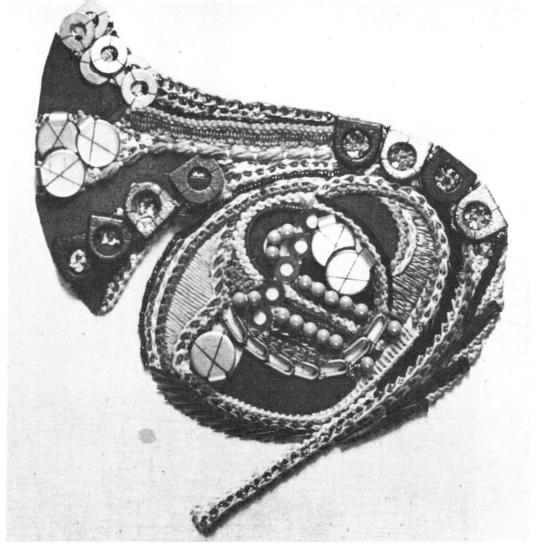

Conclusion

French Horn, Andrea
Hazell (17).

When you design for, or work, embroidery, try to keep an open mind. Do not think of the craft just as the execution of neat stitchery. Combine all the aspects of the medium that you have learnt from this book. Drawing, pattern making and the choice of fabric, colour, threads and suitable stitchery, all have their part to play in a successful piece of work. Always remember to consider carefully the function of whatever you are making and whether the design and method of embroidery are appropriate.

The scope of embroidery is immense and the joy is that work can be done at home with the minimum of inexpensive equipment.

The most important point of all, is to enjoy yourself in whatever aspect of the subject you choose to follow.

62

Suppliers Addresses

Embroidery threads etc.	Needlewoman Shop. 146 – 148 Regent Street, London W1K 6BA.
	MacCullock & Wallis Ltd., 25 – 26 Dering Street, London W1R 0BH.
	Dryad, Northgates, Leicester LE1 4QR.
Leather – gold and silver kid	The Light Leather Company, 16 Soho Square, London W1
Leather/felt offcuts	E. Gent, 709 Blackburn Road, Bolton, Lancs.
Sculpture scrim	Alec Tiranti Ltd., 21, Goodge Place, London W1
Beads and Sequins	Ells & Farrier, 5 Princes Street, Hanover Square, London W1
Shisha Glass	Maharani Boutique, 10 Quadrant Arcade, 80 – 82 Regent Street, London W1
Thrums (long ends of unsorted yarns) usually in mixed colours	The Weavers Shop, Wilton Royal Carpet Factory, Wilton, near Salisbury, Wilts. SP2 0AY
Hand weaving and embroidery yarns	Yarns, 21 Portland Street, Taunton, TA1 1UY.
General craft materials (mail order) nets, scrim, beads, shisha glass, metal foil etc	Cotswold Craft Centre, 5 Whitehall, Stroud, Glos. GL5 1HA
Scotchguard, fabric protector	Most good department stores

Useful Books

Machine Embroidery – Technique and Design	Jennifer Gray: Batsford.
Inspiration for Embroidery	Constance Howard: Batsford.

Design in Embroidery	Kathleen Whyte: Batsford.
Simple Stitches	Anne Butler: Batsford.
100 Embroidery Stitches	J. P. Coates Ltd.
Fun with Collage	Jan Beaney: Kaye & Ward Ltd.
Introducing Quilting	Eirian Short: Batsford.

Acknowledgements

Grateful thanks and acknowledgements are due to the following for their co-operation and help in the preparation of this book:

Coats Sewing Group; The Humble Oil Refinery, Houston, Texas; Miss Lynette de Denne and The Embroiderers' Guild; Members of the 62 Group; and the teachers and students, many from the following list of schools, who have kindly allowed me to show examples of their work:

Furze Platt Junior School, Maidenhead, Berks.
Cookham Dean Primary School, Maidenhead, Berks.
St. Joseph's R.C. Primary School, Maidenhead, Berks.
Braywood C. of E. Primary School, Maidenhead, Berks.
St. Mary's R.C. Primary School, Maidenhead, Berks.
Hill Top Middle and Infant School, Stoke-on-Trent.
Dartford Technical High School, Kent.
St. Bartholomew's Infant and Junior School, Leicestershire.
Gillingham Technical School, Kent.
Rushcliffe Comprehensive School, Nottingham.
Prendegast Grammar School, London.
St. Mary's Grammar School, Middlesex.
Newlands School, Cumberland.

Photographs by Alan Wysman, D. A. E. Taylor M.A., Lawrence Gresswell, Kenneth de Denne, and by kind permission of the Victoria and Albert Museum.

Embroidery on cover by Deborah Udall (11).